PUPPY HOUSE TRAINING

The Ultimate step-by-step Guild To House Training Your Puppy.

BRADLEY ALFRED

Table of Contents

CHAPTER ONE

INTRODUCTION

Residence education your domestic dog is ready consistency, endurance, and high-quality reinforcement. The aim is to instill properly conduct and build a loving bond along with your puppy.

It commonly takes 4-6 months for a domestic dog to be absolutely residence skilled, but a few dogs may also take in to a year. Size may be a predictor. For instance, smaller breeds have smaller bladders and higher metabolisms and require more frequent journeys out of doors. Your puppy's preceding residing situations are every other predictor. You can discover which you want to assist your puppy damage old behavior for you to set up greater applicable ones.

And even as you are education, don't worry if there are setbacks. So long as you retain management software that includes taking domestic dog out at the primary sign he desires to go and imparting him rewards, he'll study.

Experts advise which you begin house schooling your puppy whilst he is between 12 weeks and 16 weeks antique. At that factor, he has sufficient manipulate of his bladder and bowel actions to learn how to maintain it.

In case your puppy is older than 12 weeks while you bring him domestic and he's been disposing of in a cage (and in all likelihood eating his waste), house schooling may additionally take longer. You ought to reshape the canine's conduct with encouragement and praise.

CHAPTER TWO

STEPS FOR HOUSETRAINING YOUR PUPPY

Experts recommend confining the puppy to a described area, whether or not that means in a crate, in a room, or on a leash. As your pup learns that he wishes to head outdoor to do his business, you can progressively deliver him more freedom to roam about the house.

When you begin to residence train,

Follow these steps:

- Preserve the puppy on a everyday feeding agenda and get rid of his food among food.

- Take pup out to take away first element within the morning after which as soon as every half-hour to an hour. Additionally, constantly take him out of doors after meals or whilst he wakes from a sleep. Make sure he is going out remaining component at night time and before he's left alone.

- Take pup to the identical spot every time to do his enterprise. His fragrance will activate him to head.

- Stay with him outdoor, at the least until he's house trained.

- When your doggy gets rid of out of doors, reward him or give him a deal with. A walk across the community is a pleasing reward.

The usage of a Crate to residence educate doggy

A crate may be an amazing concept for house training your domestic dog, as a minimum within the short time period. It'll let you keep an eye fixed on him for symptoms he desires to go and teach him to hold it until you open the crate and permit him outdoor. Right here are a few pointers for

Using a crate:

• make sure it's miles big sufficient for the pup to stand, flip round, and lie down, but not huge sufficient for him to apply a corner as a lavatory.

• if you are the usage of the crate for more than hours at a time, make sure puppy has sparkling water, preferably in a dispenser you could connect to the crate.

• If you couldn't be home in the course of the residence schooling length, make certain any individual else offers him a spoil within the center of the day for the first 8 months.

- Don't use a crate if doggy is putting off in it. Eliminating in the crate could have several meanings: he might also have delivered terrible conduct from the refuge or pet save in which he lived earlier than; he won't be getting outdoor enough; the crate may be too huge; or he may be too younger to preserve it in.

Signs and symptoms that your puppy desires to take away

Whining, circling, sniffing, barking, or, in case your doggy is unconfined, barking or scratching on the door, are all signs he wishes to head. Take him out proper away.

House schooling Setbacks

Accidents are common in puppies as much as 12 months vintage. The motives for injuries range from incomplete house training to a trade within the puppy's surroundings.
When your pup does have a coincidence, keep on schooling. Then if it nevertheless doesn't appear to be working, seek advice from a veterinarian to rule out a medical difficulty.

CHAPTER THREE

THINGS TO DO AND DON'T IN HOUSE TRAINING YOUR PUPPY

Preserve the following do's and don'ts in mind at the same time as housetraining your domestic dog:

•	Punishing your puppy for having a twist of fate is a definite no-no. It teaches your doggy to fear you.

•	If you catch your domestic dog within the act, clap loudly so he is aware of he's completed something unacceptable. Then take him out of doors by way of calling him or taking him gently by using the collar. Whilst he's finished, reward him or deliver him a small treat.

• If you observed the evidence but didn't see the act, don't react angrily with the aid of yelling or rubbing his nose in it. Dogs aren't intellectually capable of connecting your anger with their twist of fate.

• Staying out of doors longer with pup may assist to decrease injuries. He may additionally want the more time to discover.

• Easy up accidents with an enzymatic cleaner in place of an ammonia-based totally purifier to reduce odors that might attract the puppy lowers back to the identical spot.

Dogs are simply a number of the maximum lovely matters on the earth. Parenting a brand new puppy, but, is not any walk inside the park. Right here's a manual to help you take care of the new addition to the own family.

Whilst the time comes to ultimately bring your new domestic dog domestic for the primary time, you may pretty tons anticipate 3 things: unbridled pleasure, cleaning up your domestic dog's accidents, and a major way of life adjustment. As you'll soon learn, a growing puppy desires plenty more than a meals bowl and a doghouse to thrive. And whilst it is able to be lots of work to start with, it's well worth the effort. Organizing good and wholesome behavior in the ones first few sleep-disadvantaged weeks will lay the inspiration for many canine-years of happiness for you and your doggy.

1. Discover a precise Vet

The first place you and your new domestic dog have to pass together is, you guessed it, instantly to the vet for a checkup. This visit will now not only assist ensure that your puppy is healthy and freed from serious health troubles, beginning defects, and many others., however it'll assist you take the first steps towards an awesome preventive health ordinary. In case you don't have a vet already, ask pals for guidelines. If to procure your canine from a shelter, ask their recommendation as they'll have veterinarians they swear by using. Local dog walkers and groomers are also a tremendous supply of thoughts.

2. Make the most of Your First Vet visit

Ask your vet which domestic dog ingredients he or she recommends, how often to feed, and what component length to offer your doggy.

3. Installation of vaccination plan with your vet.

4. Speak safe alternatives for controlling parasites, both external and internal.

5. Examine which signs and symptoms of illness to watch for in the course of your domestic dog's first few months.

6. Ask about when you ought to spay or neuter your dog.

7. Establish a lavatory ordinary

due to the fact puppies don't take kindly to carrying diapers, housetraining speedy becomes a excessive priority on maximum puppy proprietors' list of have to-research hints. In step with the professionals, your most potent allies in the quest to housetrain your pup are persistence, planning, and lots of fine reinforcement. Further, it's likely not a bad idea to put a carpet-cleaning battle plan in location, because accidents will happen.

Till your pup has had all of her vaccinations, you'll need to find a place outside that's inaccessible to other animals. This enables lessen

the spread of viruses and sickness.
ensure to give lots of high quality
reinforcement each time your
domestic dog manages to potty out
of doors and, almost similarly
crucial, refrain from punishing her
when she has accidents indoors.
Understanding whilst to take your
doggy out is almost as important
as giving her praise whenever she
does take away outdoors. Right
here's a list of the maximum
common instances to take your
pup out to potty.

1.   Whilst you wake up.

2.   Proper earlier than bedtime.

3.	Right away after your domestic dog eats or drinks loads of water.

4.	When your pup wakes up from a snooze.

5.	at some point of and after bodily pastime.

6. Look ahead to Early signs and

CHAPTER FOUR

SYMPTOMS OF CONTAMINATION

For the primary few months, puppies are extra liable to unexpected bouts of ailments that may be severe if now not stuck within the early stages. In case you observe any of the subsequent signs and symptoms to your puppy, it's time to touch the vet.

1. Loss of urge for food
2. Negative weight gain
3. Vomiting
4. Swollen of painful stomach
5. Lethargy (tiredness)

6.   Diarrhea

7.   Difficulty respiration

8.   Wheezing or coughing

9.   Pale gums

10.   Swollen, crimson eyes or eye discharge

11.   Nasal discharge

12.   Lack of ability to skip urine or stool

6. Train Obedience

By means of teaching your puppy proper manners, you'll set your doggy up for a life of advantageous social interaction. Similarly, obedience education will help forge a stronger bond among you and your domestic dog.

coaching your doggy to obey instructions which include sit, live, down, and are available will not best galvanize your friends, however these instructions will assist keep your dog secure and underneath manipulate in any potentially risky conditions. Many pup owners find that obedience lessons are a wonderful manner to teach each proprietor and dog. Training usually starts accepting puppies at age 4 to 6 months.

THE END